IN THE NET

IN THE NET

Hawad

Translated from French by Christopher Wise
Translated from Tuareg (Tamajaght) into French
by the poet and Hélène Claudot-Hawad
Foreword by Hélène Claudot-Hawad

University of Nebraska Press / Lincoln

Originally published as *Dans la nasse* © 2014 by Non Lieu

"Foreword to the French Language Edition" (as "Preface") and
excerpts of chapters 2–4 previously appeared in "Scribes, Griots,
Poets: New Writings from West Africa," ed. Susanne Paola Antonetta,
special issue, *Bellingham Review* 42, no. 80 (Spring 2020): 60–70.

The University of Nebraska Press is part of a land-grant institution
with campuses and programs on the past, present, and future
homelands of the Pawnee, Ponca, Otoe-Missouria, Omaha, Dakota,
Lakota, Kaw, Cheyenne, and Arapaho Peoples, as well as those
of the relocated Ho-Chunk, Sac and Fox, and Iowa Peoples.

The African Poetry Book Series has been made possible
through the generosity of philanthropists Laura and Robert
F. X. Sillerman, whose contributions have facilitated the
establishment and operation of the African Poetry Book Fund.

Library of Congress Cataloging-in-Publication Data
Names: Hawad, author. | Wise, Christopher, 1961– translator. |
Claudot-Hawad, Hélène, translator, writer of foreword.
Title: In the net / Hawad ; translated from French by Christopher
Wise ; translated from Tuareg (Tamajaght) into French by the poet
and Hélène Claudot-Hawad ; foreword by Hélène Claudot-Hawad.
Description: Lincoln : University of Nebraska Press,
[2022] | Series: African poetry book series
Identifiers: LCCN 2021022938
ISBN 9781496229694 (paperback)
ISBN 9781496230171 (epub)
ISBN 9781496230188 (pdf)
Subjects: LCSH: Hawad—Translations into English. |
BISAC: POETRY / African | LCGFT: Poetry.
Classification: LCC PJ2381.9.H39 I5 2022 | DDC 893/.38—dc23
LC record available at https://lccn.loc.gov/2021022938

Set in Garamond Premier by Laura Buis.
Designed by N. Putens.

CONTENTS

FOREWORD

Hélène Claudot-Hawad

Translating Hawad's poetry presents several challenges to overcome. The first is linguistic and political by implication. The others are paralinguistic, semantic, and stylistic. Throughout this process, Hawad's double role as author and co-translator enables significant freedom of choice in transferring the text from one language to another.

WHAT DOES IT MEAN FOR AFRICANS TO WRITE IN THEIR MOTHER TONGUES?

Tamajaght is the language of the Imajaghen—Tuareg for "those on the outside"—a people who live in the central Sahara and along the shores of the desert.[1] This language, which is associated with a particularly rich oral literature, belongs to the Amazigh, or Berber, linguistic family. It is also endowed with a very ancient form of writing: tifinagh, whose geometric inscriptions have been engraved or painted on rock across the Saharan region since prehistoric times.

If Hawad chooses to write in his own language, Tamajaght, which he transcribes with the tifinagh alphabet, he does so in a very particular political context: that of the African nation-states created in the 1960s. At the end of Africa's so-called independence process, the Tuareg people found themselves divided between five nation-states. On the one hand, the Sahelian states (Mali, Niger, and present-day Burkina Faso) adopted French, the language of the colonizer, as their official language. On the other hand, the Mediterranean states (Libya, Algeria) opted for Arabic, thereby disassociating themselves from Africa to become the "West" (Maghreb) of the Muslim capital (Mecca).

That is why, in the 1970s, younger Tuareg (Imajaghen) who were forced into political and economic exile wrote in Tamajaght in the tifinagh alphabet, thus mobilizing this form of writing as a means of resistance. In the written letters they circulate and in their political diatribes, they have intensified their use of this writing by vocalizing the consonantal tifinagh alphabet to make their texts easier to read. Hawad is one of the initiators of this trend.[2] To hew an acceptable path through an aggressive "modernity," they seized the cultural tools that were bequeathed to them by their ancestors and adapted them to entirely new uses. State rule in the Sahara indeed seeks to abolish lifestyles, policies, and economies that are outside its control. In the new states where the Tuareg live, nomadic mobility has become illegal. Amazigh languages and tifinagh were legally banned in the Maghreb for nearly half a century, and Islamists continue to oppose them today. During the 1970s and 1980s, authorities in the Arab states repeatedly confiscated Hawad's manuscripts. Under Hawad's pen, these manuscripts, written in vocalized tifinagh, developed into a cursive form. But censorship will never keep Hawad from writing, for, as he says, "When speech is stifled, the audience fragmented, and the mobility of men and their ideas obstructed, writing in Tamajaght is, first and foremost, a way to push beyond limits, to circumvent confinement, to ricochet the echoes in my landscapes and build new spaces for thinking, feeling and speaking the world differently."[3]

A MINIMIZED LANGUAGE AND ABSENT DICTIONARIES

The lack of linguistic tools, due to cultural policies of new nation-states, is yet another aspect of the political minoritization of Tamajaght: there is no monolingual dictionary of the Tamajaght language, no thesaurus, no semantic lexicon, no elaborate grammatical study, no extensive bilingual dictionary other than the Tuareg-French dictionary of Father Charles de Foucauld, a Christian missionary at the time of the French occupation of the Sahara in the early twentieth century. Given its basis in colonialist ideology, de Foucauld's dictionary draws from the terminology of material existence, not the abstract terminology of Tuareg thought and imagination. Hence, it is no help for the translation of a poetry like Hawad's.

Beyond the challenge of conveying a particular cultural imagination into the host language, one that is born of the desert, the translator must also render a wholly original style that deconstructs the original language through disrupting the usual lexicon and syntax. This poetry of collision and shock corresponds to the present chaotic situation and to the quest to find new ways to think the world otherwise:

> I see writing not only as a weapon but as an anchor to drag along, a black trail giving weight and consistency to the march of the resistance, as it pursues its own goals. In sum, writing is memory but without being confined to the past: It is a tether unwound from the abyss, an act that nourishes, like the well animal that draws water from the ground to irrigate the thirsty deserts of the unknown. Writing is a gesture resituating the margins at the center of the world's matrix.[4]

In the case of his own poetic imagination, Hawad evokes the notion of *tikruru*. In Tamajaght, this term refers to an individual who is able to establish a link between several distinct cultures and thereby achieve an original synthesis from a variety of different sources. Hawad defines himself as a tikruru. As a polyglot who is no stranger to cultural diversity and as an intercontinental traveler, he is stimulated by diverse languages, alternative conceptual universes, and different ways of living and conceiving the world. For Hawad, the whole is a creative ferment that he values and presses into service. This is the perspective from which he links translation to the universe of *takrur*, an intercultural space where all roads can meet and interconnect. Although medieval historians in the Sahel commonly attributed the term Takrur to a people or a land, the Tamajaght meaning of this word in a broader sense refers to the state of cultural *métissage* and synthesis allowing individuals to understand and master the codes of several different universes while remaining comfortable in each. Translation interests Hawad as a singular encounter propelling the text elsewhere, into unforeseen spaces, and that builds unlikely bridges between worlds that are not accustomed to interacting or being situated alongside one another.

In his own poetry, Hawad breaks with the classical registers of Tuareg poetry. He asserts the free character of his writings against older literary forms. His volcanic poetry deliberately provokes short circuits in sound, diction, meaning, and imagination. The question for the translator then becomes how to replicate the explosive impact of these unprecedented encounters, how to capture the movement and emotional turbulence that the text produces when so many opposing notions collide. It is not sufficient to fasten upon words alone. One must also rediscover the idea that is latent within the text, what the strangeness of the idea might awaken in the target language, how it might disrupt its established order, its semantic, lexical, and syntactic certainties. Even if it means abandoning certain words during the transfer, the final result must disrupt the target language in the same way that the original text disrupts the source language. The poetic must resonate in such a way that it will enable the exploration of the unexplored margins of the self. The birthing of a new language from this transfer must cause the imaginary world that is imprisoned within its own identity to vibrate. For the Tuareg, *this* is the meaning of *takrur*.

TRANSLATION CHOICES

In concrete terms, we adopted several strategies in translating from Tamajaght into French. In the original manuscript, Hawad's text appears as a continuum in which the position of the words is wholly reversible. This means that each word relates to whatever comes before it or after it. In the original language text, the almost total absence of punctuation amplifies the polycentric link between words. French is less flexible. The implacability of gender and number agreement (especially in the case of articles) often prohibits such an open relationship to develop between words. To preserve the flexibility of the original text, we didn't always punctuate it and we eliminated a number of articles. We also used line breaks to mark the breaths for the oral reading of Hawad's poetry, which is the only real way to get a sense of its rapid pace and frenetic rhythm. A sense of collision is created through the juxtaposing of nouns. In ordinary French, if articles were added to nouns and connecting prepositions, it would break up the momentum of the whole. These linguistic elements are eliminated here to restore the rhythmic vigor of the original text.

There are a number of key concepts in Hawad's manuscript that have no satisfactory equivalents in French, a difficulty inherent in any translation:

To cite one instance, the Tuareg noun *iman* is commonly translated as "soul" [*l'âme*] in the philosophical sense of the term—in other words, "that which feels, thinks, and desires within us"—without any religious connotation. Translating this term in such a way doesn't exhaust the meaning of *iman* as a plural noun that refers to a dynamic conception of realities that are perceived in motion. The plural form conveys the impermanent state of things due to their constant transformation into something else. At the same time, this word designates the most intimate part of the self, the personality, our interiority, the soul as enmeshed within the more ephemeral aspects of life. In the Tuareg imagination, several components of the "soul" correspond with the four founding cosmic elements: earth, water, air, and fire. That is why, depending on the context, *iman* may also be translated differently ("self," essence, being, soul, the soul state [*le 'soi,' l'essence, l'être, l'âme, l'état d'âme*]).[5]

A TRANSLATION SHOULD BE A BRIDGE

In our translation work, we found some affinities with the ground-breaking remarks of the French traveler and writer Chateaubriand (1768–1809) in his translation of Milton's *Paradise Lost*. Chateaubriand's goal wasn't to create an "elegant translation" (i.e., a normalizing translation of the original poetic work) but a "literal" translation that did not reduce the text to the logic of the host language. Chateaubriand didn't hesitate to recreate certain English phrases in French in order to preserve their originality to "introduce the [French] reader to the genius of the English language."[6]

This approach is close to the notion of deterritorializing a text, preserving what is most original about it but also imposing the unexplored possibilities of the host language. This way of saying things otherwise can belong to any imaginative construct; doing so compels us to expand our vision of the world, inciting every language imprisoned within its own identity, its own unique logic and normality, to vibrate. For Hawad, this is where the true poetry of translation resides, suggesting there are other ways and other means of perceiving the world. A translation should be a bridge rather than the exclusive property of one language. Its value lies in the way it obliges languages to pulsate beyond their own sounds and their own resonances. Like poetry, translation has the ability to free language from its shackles, to make language sufficiently elastic and plastic so that new meanings and new horizons might be accommodated within it. This is the sense in which translation becomes tikruru. As the Tuareg say, *tikruru* is like "the point of a needle connecting both edges of the cloth without taking the color of either."

NOTES

1. Depending on the accent, Tamajaght is also pronounced Tamahaght, Tamashaght, or even Tamazight.

2. Hawad, "L'élite que nous avons voulu raccommoder sur les cendres ... après la création des États africains" [An elite that we hoped to forge from the ashes ... after the creation of the African states], *Nomadic Peoples* 2, nos. 1–2 (1998): 84–102.

3. Hawad, oral statement, Barcelona 2003, quoted in Hélène Claudot-Hawad, "Les tifinagh comme écriture du détournement: Usages touaregs du XXIe siècle" [Tifinagh as a writing that reroutes: Tuareg practices of the twenty-first century], *Etudes et Documents Berbères*, no. 23 (2005): 5–30, https://hal.ird.fr/AC/halshs-00293892v1.

4. Interview with Bernard Bretonnière in Hawad, Hélène Claudot-Hawad, and Bernard Bretonnière, *Buveurs de braise* [Ember drinkers] (Saint-Nazaire, France: MEET, 1995).

5. Hélène Claudot-Hawad, prelude to *Vent Rouge* [Red wind], by Hawad (Paris: Éditions de l'Institut du Tout-Monde, 2020).

6. Chateaubriand, "Remarques," in *Le Paradis perdu* [*Paradise Lost*], by John Milton, trans. Chateaubriand (Paris: Ed. Belin, 1990), 27.

TRANSLATOR'S NOTE

Christopher Wise

I have been reading Hawad for almost three decades and have also translated many Sahelian writers during that time. After the conflict in northern Mali in 2012–13, I felt Hawad's response to Azawad was something I needed to understand. Though I have studied Sahelian literature for many years, I don't speak Hawad's language, Tamajaght. Hélène Claudot-Hawad is fluent in Tamajaght and also speaks English. Hence, Hélène played an indispensable role in the production of the English language translation of this poem.

Hélène and I began the translation process in July 2019. I translated two chapters of Hawad's poem into English at that time and sent the translation to Hélène and Hawad. I did the early translation work in Sun Valley, Idaho, not far from Ezra Pound's birthplace and Ernest Hemingway's gravesite. It's a wonderful place to write.

After I sent the first two chapters to Hélène and Hawad, I was dismayed to find they wanted many changes. Some of the changes seemed to reflect a bias toward British English rather than American vernacular English. So, I told Hélène that American poets don't follow Shakespeare; they follow Whitman. This led to some wrangling over diction, idioms, and so on. After completing the first few chapters, I put the translation on hold knowing I would be in Paris in February 2020. I decided to take a trip to Aix-en-Provence at that time to meet with Hawad and Hélène in person and see if we couldn't work through our disagreements.

We had a wonderful meeting, in large part due to Hawad and Hélène's hospitality, and I felt I better understood what was happening on their end: Hélène and Hawad went through every single word of the poem in translation. They wanted to make sure the translation was true to Hawad's original meaning. Although Hawad doesn't speak English, Hélène explained each word and line to him. This means it wasn't just Hélène who weighed in and made suggestions for the English language translation. Hawad, too, was involved in the creative process.

After my visit with Hawad, I left the meeting in awe of him. He is quite simply one of the most impressive persons I've ever met. My daughter Ayesha and her friend Charlaey came to the luncheon that Hawad himself prepared for us. He showed us his atelier where he writes and creates his tifinagh artwork. (My daughter Ayesha made a brief film of our meeting, "Hawad's Atelier in Provence," which is posted on my YouTube channel.)[1] After lunch, Hawad and I had a lively discussion on the Tuareg notions *takrur* and *tikruru*. I was already familiar with the Takrur region (in northern Senegal, what the French later renamed as the Saint Louis District but which is better known in Senegal as the Futa Tooro). Much of my research in the past has been based in the Takrur region of Senegal, especially Alwaar, the birthplace of Al Hajj Umar Taal. Takrur was also the name of an old kingdom, older than even the Songhay dynasty but related to the Songhay dynasty, as the Askiya Muhammad and the Songhay (or Wakuri) nobility originally came to Gao and Timbuktu from the Takrur.

What I didn't know was the relevance of this term for the Tuareg people, albeit with a meaning I'd never encountered before. For Hawad and the Tuareg, *takrur* refers to a dynamic process of transformation that occurs during translation, a process commonly enacted by the Tuareg, who often find themselves in situations where they must translate different languages and cultures into their own idioms. Hawad and I discussed the idea of *takrur* at length in relation to Sahelian authors I'd previously translated, and also after I suggested to him that, for an American poet like Pound, a translated poem is a unique poem in its own right. Hawad fully agreed, and this is how I learned that, for the Tuareg people, *takrur* implies far more than a geographical location in northern Senegal.

After our meeting, the translation of the remaining chapters went far more smoothly. I would send the first draft of my translation to Hélène and Hawad, written in my American English. I didn't always get what I wanted, but I knew that Hawad would get the translation *he* wanted, and this is how things should be. We continued to negotiate over almost every word in the poem until we arrived at a final draft that was acceptable to all parties. The process lasted from March through July 2020, or about five months of exchanges from Aix-en-Provence to Bellingham, Washington.

In October 2020, I returned to Sun Valley, Idaho, to translate Hélène's preface and write my own, about a mile from the lodge where Hemingway wrote *For Whom the Bell Tolls*. I note this in passing because Hemingway's novel about the Spanish Civil War was not *l'art pour l'art* but an epic intended to stir his readers to action. Hawad's poem, too, is an epic of war that is a call to action, a revolt against a situation that is intolerable. Like Hemingway's novel, Hawad's poem demands an urgent response from us.

I would like to thank my old mentor Georg M. Gugelberger, who introduced me to Hawad's poetry. I would also like to thank Susanne Paola Antonetta, editor of the *Bellingham Review* and kind *yenta* to the English-language publication of this poem, as well as Kwame Dawes for his provocative questions about its translation. Above all, I would like to thank Hélène and Hawad for their warmth and hospitality.

NOTE

1. Ayesha Wise, "Hawad's Atelier in Provence," February 27, 2020, YouTube video, https://www.youtube.com/watch?v=cAOHzDRLB-I.

In the first line of this new work with its revealing title, Hawad inscribes three enigmatic letters, "Z, T, alpha" (ⵣ+ⵣ in tifinagh, the writing of the Tuareg) for, he says, "Letters are pillars for us that are more solid than the mountains. The vowel Alpha incarnates the ability to pass from one state to another, to energize things, whereas consonants are fixed." To begin the work of transforming Tuareg pain and loosening up the nets that ensnare them, Hawad presses into service a unique alchemy of letters and other "furigraphic" techniques, making sounds, words, and images collide together with the goal of re-instigating movement, a surge forth, or "swarm" of activity, in an immobile and no-win situation.

This text, completed in March 2013, was written at the height of the Azawad revolt that began early in 2012 and during France's military intervention in 2013. These events culminated in the violent reinstallation of Mali's crumbling army and its failed state in the Sahara, assuring the oblivion of the Tuareg people. In face of so much amnesia, how to live? How to make an alternative voice heard amid the cacophony of media-generated accounts of terrorism, fearmongering, the roar of the fighter jets, the proliferation of drones in the Sahara, the massacre of civilians, state-monitored terminology, and unchecked imperialist discourse clarifying the good and evil parties in this conflict?

For Hawad, the emergence of Azawad obliterated what was most essential about a century-old fight, the struggle of a people to liberate themselves from colonial and neocolonial rule. If he speaks directly to Azawad in this text, it is as a part of himself—that is, as the Tuareg that he is—but a part that has endured so much suffering, misery, oppression that it no longer contests the erasure that is inherent in the labels assigned to it. It is by way of this evanescent character, hovering on the brink of the abyss, deprived of speech, room for movement, the right to exist, that Hawad seeks to piece back together a silhouette figure, one that might have lost its arms, legs, and tongue but remains still capable of picking itself up off the ground, of transposing itself to a different sphere and a more acceptable horizon. He strikes a new path amid the rubble of the fire that destroyed the old path, sending out smoke signals to this blackened figure, metamorphosing its suffering into a compost of resistance, a resistance of a wholly other sort, one that requires this figure to come back to itself, to the resources of its imagination, to attempt to think the world otherwise, and not through the lens of those who refuse it the right to exist.

The road will be long. Hawad uses poetry as a resistance weapon, "cartridges of old words, / a thousand and one misfires, botched, reloaded." He assigns names to the Tuareg body in its varying stages of decomposition as well as the mining companies that are behind its destruction and dismemberment:

> The skull is at In Amenas [Camel Skull]
> but the brain of the Camel Ancestor
> transformed into combustible
> gas oil fuel
> flows in the furrow streams
> gorges of our defeats,
> beyond the desert and the sea.
> And it turns fertilizer for lard hills
> grease heaps,
> states with army and obese joints,
> disaster!

He scrapes out the wounds of defeat and makes them bleed anew to provoke a fresh reaction, to reanimate this paralyzed body, to restore its lucid gaze:

But when you are flesh
skewered in a circle of fire,
you must know how to stare at the flames.

The goal is to be able to look clearly at the situation and to adopt an appropriate critical distance:

Disgust,
Azawad,
spit from up high like a camel
but aim well, spit on the right enemy eye!
A guerilla must know how choose his target
and ration his ammo!

Everything that is a source of pain is explicitly enunciated, like the loneliness of the Tuaregs

You're alone, Azawad,
without guns or ammo
no allies or comrades in sight

and the denials

who wrote the manuscripts?
Who built
Timbuktu's walls?
Wasn't it the tribes Imessoufa, Imaqesharen,
Igdalen, Ilemtayen, and the Igelad,
Tuaregs

or the devastation

Faces broken mirrors,
portraits of women children old people,

land and men tossed into the flames,
on their knees in the mud
of fires at full blast

or the repetition of the colonial disaster

Disaster deprivation scarcity
plague liturgy of agonies beneath chaos
epilepsy telluric earth tremors
expropriation's litanies and rosaries
exclusions exterminations
violent avalanche procession
devastations and their suite
ricochets of our self's debris
that crash
amid other hissings from the abyss

or illusions

don't imagine you'll find a pothole
underneath the chariot's wheel,
salvation oblivion, where to rest

or compromises that serve no purpose

Don't beg for the very air
you breathe,
shake up your destiny.
Your exterminator
doesn't need your help

or technology's invasion

Today in the skies of the Sahara and Sahel,
the ravens and vultures no longer fly,
only drones and fighter jets.

Faced with so much adversity, the unequal distribution of power, and the world's indifference, Hawad writes:

With a single blast of dynamite
another nuance of existence is erased
another accent of humanity
to make way for haste business hordes
rushing to quarry
uranium mines or petrol fuel
motorways tunnels abysses
cities barracks anthills
toxic mushrooms
land seizures negation annihilation
of our existence.

He erects pillars to hold up the only roof that is solid enough to provide the Tuareg with enduring shelter, in other words, the deep-seated acceptance of themselves as Tuaregs:

Beyond yourself, there's no
surrogate Tuareg
for you to hide behind.

To forge a path through the flames, he makes use of poetic hallucinations,

awkward exhalation
wing, breath,
flashover butterfly
for emotion's epileptic gasps

spanning storms waves flames
chaos anomie devastation.

He spells out passwords to find the right path once again: "You yourself are the beacon, / lone witness" and to face "the ascent of deserts and mirages / is your heritage, yours alone." He "shackles the yoke" by going beyond today's horizon

in alluring dream gaze
eternal landscape
blue horizon without end
land beyond land
venerated, dream.

To see beyond the limits of the gaze is a recurrent theme in Hawad's writings, where only the blind and the mad seem endowed with the gift of clairvoyance. The goal is to think beyond the narrow confines of the established order, to renounce the categories restricting the Tuareg, and to dismantle dominant grammatical forms in order to see himself in his own eyes:

Azawad, be obstinate.
Hold on,
bite into the fibers of your imagination.
And let go of the illusory folklore
of human zoos.

For, as the author tirelessly reminds us in his works,

to be defeated is an art
mastered in solitude
in the dark of night.

Noise and the drumbeat of words, explosions, outbursts, fury, and derision characterize the words that the reader will find in these pages: rapid breathing, gasps for air, curt interjections, irony, and caustic humor culminate in abolishing the rhythms of ordinary speech, making punctuation useless, exploding the logic of the oppressive discourse that would condemn entire worlds to disappearance. But condemned by whom? A violent flood of images surges forth, expediential in force, sweeping away every pre-established category to sketch out new paths, alternative landscapes, other horizons at the end of a hard march. Hawad labors diligently to bring what is now invisible and unimaginable into full view, scaling the highest mountain pass with the widest vista, at long last freed of fetters.

ACKNOWLEDGMENTS

Our warmest thanks to Christopher Wise for his intellectual openness, patience, and efforts that enabled our perspectives on translating from Tamajaght to French, and from French to English, to be so eloquently discussed. Thanks also to his daughter Ayesha, who succeeded in giving an idea of our meeting by filming it so sensitively. Warm thanks also to Christiane Fioupou, a translator and specialist in English-speaking African literature, for her invaluable help. Finally, thanks to Kwame Dawes for his inspired questions that have been so stimulating for us.

HAWAD, INK I

HAWAD, INK 2

HAWAD, INK 3

HAWAD, INK 4

HAWAD, INK 5

IN THE NET

I

Z, T, alpha.
Oh Azawad!
Where is Aïr, Ahaggar, Azawagh,
Adghagh of the Idemakan, and Ajjer,
mountains rocks spines
basis of our endurance?

Oh bodies souls
burnt quartered
ashes and dust.
Azawad,
I'm not seeking
help, pity for you me,
the man they bleed's already dead!

Azawad,
you me wade through
in the slurry manure of the same hell.
I'm not asking you
to stab your own chest.
But when you are flesh
skewered in a circle of fire,
you must know how to stare at the flames.

Grab your solitude
nerve of our pain.
Azawad, don't groan!
What you must fear is the end of self.

Death's whistle has sounded,
genocide, extermination.
The goal is already achieved.
Let's talk instead about resurrection.

Disaster deprivation scarcity
plague liturgy of agonies beneath chaos
epilepsy telluric earth tremors
expropriation's litanies and rosaries
exclusions exterminations
violent avalanche procession
devastations and their suite
ricochets of our self's debris
that crash
amid other hissings from the abyss
to once again rely on
in the tutor of the infinite
the end's new beginnings,
grinding and sieving
on the ogre's behalf.

Azawad,
your persist breath,
is an affront,
you, the residue
of machine gun and machete,
you're always on the move,
irritating witness to your own death.
All the wretched noise
and tumult that engulfs you
is but the echo,
spate of the beginnings,
new endings.
The true end,

before you were even born,
has done riding your soul,
you who've already disappeared,
dead, but still disturbing the eyes of
your assassin.

Azawad, desert
dead in its shroud,
tunic of your parents,
Tuareg,
for a longtime your people
have been hurled headlong
into the abyss
where there are
only a few skinny goat's kids
us you me,
scapegoats force-fed with
gunpowder sulfur gasoline
for the great day
of carnival carnage-game.

After your flaying, the lord of the carnival
gathered all he had at Timbuktu,
of necks boots bullets
from Africa and Europe,
drums artillery
of the humiliations and massacres
that set his boot back in the stirrup,
iron horse hooves stainless steel.
Chaos amok in the land.
Shelling strafing explosions scree.
Heads and guts tumble,
torrents in the waves
of radioactive surf.

The cyclone atomic screen
armor plate iron rampart.
Iron arches weld
on fire's rims.
Arc cycle iron fire closes
in a circuit of reprisals.
And cinders,
carbon 14 for nothing,
not even history,
are thrust open in the barren orifice
of zero.

Azawad,
we're stuck in the rumen,
swamp geography
of volcanic furnaces.
Don't whine about it!
No heart wants to touch you.
Endure, Azawad!
Chaos is ours.
Spare our tears and feelings.

Ember nerves,
like the desert
your homeland,
you tremble with fever,
you burn, Azawad.
Vein, flames' sap
your fossil arteries run dry,
burst open to irrigate uranium
rocks and hippopotamuses with snouts
for mineral truffles.

2

Azawad,
chew your blindfold,
gnaw at the darkness
and stare at the obvious.
Faces broken mirrors,
portraits of women children old people,
land and men tossed into the flames,
on their knees in the mud
of fires at full blast.

Hunger thirst in your gut
stuffed with bullets flint,
provisions for the journey
beyond the tombstone.
In the desert of the Tuaregs,
there is gold oil coal gas
and dreadful uranium,
and solitude
before lawlessness and abuse.

A busy bee,
your disarmed gaze.
Eclipsed.
Your gaze must be put out,
your gaze, Azawad.
Your existence disrupts.
The judges have no need
of your testimony.

Order is order
and truth another matter.
No need for Tuaregs
to watch over the Sahara.
Hunting ground beaters stampede,
open season on "the reds."

Timbuktu Gao Kidal
Tchin Tabaraden Agadez In Gall
Tamanrasset Ghat Ghadames,
sand air underground resources,
Sahara wreckage,
the horizon tent
of the Tuaregs collapses
under a niqab of shrapnel and bombs.

Silence!
Even silence is speechless.
And the survivors and the dead are crushed,
so are herds valleys mountains and plains,
from the turrets of the automated tanks
machine gun grenade flamethrowers
and soldiers flanked by auxiliary forces,
blanket of bullets and cannons,
swarming helicopters,
mirages drones fighter jets
gringos frogs.
Today in the skies of the Sahara and Sahel,
the ravens and vultures no longer fly,
only drones and fighter jets.

The day before yesterday, Azawad,
they turned you into a guinea pig for their atomic fire.

Now, they stone you to death with their bombs
mortar arrows made from your uranium in Arlit,
depleted into terror.
Terror that destroys not only
the "evil Islamist terrorists"
in horrifying deaths
calcinating and atomizing them,
but that also turns all living things into ash
anything alive
daring to breath in the Sahara.

Azawad,
don't cry.
This time you'll die
a highly efficient death
without tears or witnesses,
a cutting-edge death,
charred flesh
with no need for cremation in gas chambers.
The bulldozers and motion sensors
of Areva, of Sonatrach in Algiers, atomic China
and the other multinationals will dig
vast mass graves
for you and your like.
Don't feel sorry for yourself
don't cry out, "No! It can't be true!
I'm screwed! Azawad is screwed!"
Throughout the plains dunes valleys
and in your gutted torn stolen mountains
the ghost the shadows in exile of your sisters
crawl exhausted, dragging heavy balls of agony,
on the ashes and smoldering embers
crackling with your brothers.

Azawad, don't ask me for the key
or bullet to liberation.
I have only cartridges of old words,
a thousand and one misfires, botched, reloaded.
Cough, rage, bitterness.
Ugh! I vomit the strangled flight of furigraphic revolt.

3

Azawad,
you must still gird
your memory.
In the north of Ajjer
to Tin Gantouren, stump land
your people's skeletons,
Algerian explosives and their masks
blew up the mausoleum sepulchers
of the martyrs and their masks
to secure the foundations
of their gas factory.

Your martyrs
by voice of bones and shards
resounding death rattles
pain deception
deaf and cold complaint,
complaint of the forgotten,
awake sleep.
The sacrificed bind the throat in lava
magma of annulled memories,
whetted tone wailings
distressed sounds redoubling
the chorus and the echo's call.
But the voice of shards and bones won't
blend associate or mingle with the crowd
panic concert uproar
of lunatic trance powers,

that in the mausoleums
hidden in the gas factory
come face to face, in mortal combat,
soldiers and their trained dogs.
Kicks.
They kick bite aim strike one another.
Explosions insults yelps,
they bray Allahu Akbar Allahu Akbar,
Allahu is ours,
Allahu is yours,
Allahu you,
Allahu to bar.
You must attack,
attack, by God,
to bar to bar!

Rubbish, pool balls, crude lumps,
disorder obscenity's debris violence
guttural grumblings
in one-eyed Koranic Arabic
squatting and metamorphizing
places altars
in brothel butchery,
gas factory in flames.
At Tin Gantouren
what voice
of horror and fear
won't have brayed at the stump cadavers
of our fleet fighting camels
thrashed twice over?

The skull is at In Amenas [Camel Skull]
but the brain of the Camel Ancestor
transformed into combustible

gas oil fuel
flows in the furrow streams
gorges of our defeats,
beyond the desert and the sea.
And it turns fertilizer for lard hills
grease heaps,
states with army and obese joints,
disaster!

Azawad, don't say:
"Aye! Azawad, I'm beat.
Is it really me,
the mutilated and tortured Tuareg here
in search of a spare self,
some substitute slated for destruction
rather than the Tuareg
I still am?
Is there no other me that I
might curl up behind?"

This one, Azawad,
this Tuareg,
it's you,
you alone.
Beyond yourself, there's no
surrogate Tuareg
for you to hide behind.
Azawad, it's just you,
the first one,
who is exposed
under your annihilation.
The Tuareg has four souls
but none can serve as
substitutes for the others

before its turn.
After you bury the steps
of the next one, you'll make it rise again.
It's your silhouette
that gives it form and meaning.

4

Evil omens
flesh eating vultures!
This morning, the planes of war
deposited in Timbuktu
a warlord
of colonization.
Like in the days of 1890,
the time of conquest
looting inquisition forced labor,
the supreme warlord
is now drunk with self-satisfaction
finding a deluge in Timbuktu
a mob black with anger, dregs, hatred.
And the drunken mob staggers along, happy
to gulp slobber and the blood of easy prey
that it regurgitates for its master,
the self-designated messiah
Africa's pacifier.

And together they share in the victories and the accolades,
they reward their armies
their auxiliary forces and allies,
parrot griots.
And parade the booty and the prisoners,
long-eared foxes scorpions desert locust nomads
caught in the serval's trap.

All the prisoners from the desert
are sacrificed on the fetish altar
of integrity and unity of the realm.
A portion of the spoils goes to the warlord,
sovereign of the battlefield and armies.
Hostage spoils orphan,
the baby albino camel
overt sorrow thirst fear nostalgia
for the scent of his mother Tanezruft
and his dead caretaker,
red scarecrow fox
"terrorist," the bad guy who robs
the pretty pretty pacifists,
Mali with its courageous war veterans
who ran away from
forced labor and their mothers
in the great war
to liberate their Aunty Metropolis
from horrible barbaric enslavement
to her German cousins.

What happened next? War,
war is war,
the continuity of death
without consequences.
The clock is ticking
fleeting like the bullet whistling past.
The commander has neither time nor leisure
to think about the spoils of war.
He fixes his eye instead
on the true prize,
one that his troops,
who have neither the eyes nor the telescopes
for long-range viewing,

can quite make out,
the true loot that lies in the earth,
earth bereaved of water
and masters,
and the slightest compassion,
earth of desert,
earth decreed vacant.

To get a glimpse of the rich prizes
twitching in the tendons of the Sahara,
you'll need wings and a keen eye
an air force
with electronic instruments for dissection,
like a true warlord messiah
of the apocalypse.

Atteeeeeeen hut!
And the escort at the inspection
of the frontline stops,
riveted in place
by a tiny smudge of ash
three manuscripts,
three receipt ledgers
and the edicts of sharia
for cleaning testicles and phallus
and the nine holes of the body
and unlawful marriage.

5

Tornado season ululations,
hellfire sirens brimstone storms,
herald the wedding of Venus and Mars,
immaculate conception of Timbuktu.
While the excavators dredge,
the dust of the Sahara
scuttling in every direction.
Gallop, bulimia.
They crush
everything failing to interest them.
No alarm siren Madeleine
nor police for the Rights of Man
protection for the world's patrimony,
no one gives a damn
about the cries of destruction
for museums libraries art
and tifinagh writing of a thousand millennia,
as they lie in ruins.

Who bothered their heads
about the destruction of the writings, art
and cosmic visions of the Tuareg?
Not a single dog barked. The customs officer
for feelings and imagination gave a free pass
and refused to see or hear a thing,
unless it involved Timbuktu and its manuscripts
on hygiene
sharia law and the Imam Malek.

And yet, Azawad,
in the Tuareg Sahara,
even silence cries into the void.
The tattoos boo and hiss
at every lithic fresco
from Tangier to the Niger River,
from the Siwa Oasis to the Canary Islands.

Solid fixed points,
straight lines, etched zigzags,
circles and curves,
figures and enigmas
of a geometry of horizons
and infinite times,
defiant visions of the unknowable,
abyssal past or future
with the face of the unspeakable.

Rip them from every face
that exists,
no one gives a damn.
Azawad, don't forgot
that UNESCO is one of the props
of the cultural customs officials
who work for the United Nations.
And one of the edicts of the United Nations
for people without a state
is the whip.
The whip that lacerates you,
erasing every mark
of your people and your land.
No one loses any sleep over that.
You won't excite the slightest curiosity,
not even the curiosity of the cynics.

Bald indifference,
wind smoke empty dust
technological vulgarity,
censorship of the imagination
past and future
cut off, hammered to bits, erased,
like people who hold the copyright,
people without a state.
With a single blast of dynamite
another nuance of existence is erased
another accent of humanity
to make way for haste business hordes
rushing to quarry
uranium mines or petrol fuel
motorways tunnels abysses
cities barracks anthills
toxic mushrooms
land seizures negation annihilation
of our existence, everything gutted except the right
for us to imagine ourselves
otherwise.

Azawad, the mighty world belches,
bloated with vanity brutality cynicism.
Not a soul shows any dismay
or refrains from vile behavior, disgusting
bottomless greed, insatiable snouts.
Right between the world's eyelids,
bolted steel,
blocking the smallest glimmers of humanity
capable of reaching you
unless through a gun turret
or the gleam of a blade.

In this human desert,
where every gaze is a bullet
cursing the exiled
stateless people in a stolen land.
So, Azawad, shouldn't you do the same,
and stare the world down
with lucid scorn in your eyes,
and with extreme prejudice?
Disgust,
Azawad,
spit from up high like a camel
but aim well, spit on the right enemy eye!
A guerilla must know how to choose his target
and ration his ammo!
Azawad, there's no way out for you
nor alternative except within yourself,
the one who suffers
the only one who gives meaning
to your other inner selves.

6

Azawad,
in order to measure the violence,
and grasp sudden annihilation,
a lightening flash gaze is essential.
Look upon the death's head
of ruins devastation debris.
In every direction every wind,
men have vanished
with past present future substance.
They leave followed by tracks
footpaths markers wakes
memory's trails
of their visions.

Among us Tuaregs,
Azawad,
visions are a treasure
with mobile memory
navigating the horizon,
our moveable dwellings
that they have encased
in a Coke bottle
tossed aside and forgotten.
Crushing hulling grinding
shelling scraping erasing emptiness,
and never enough to make the gullies run
drivel sweat lard
leachable blood ink,

sticky beetle tears,
that the world dumps
on the clay ramparts
of Timbuktu!

Azawad,
who wrote the manuscripts?
Who built
Timbuktu's walls?
Wasn't it the tribes Imessoufa, Imaqesharen,
Igdalen, Ilemtayen, and the Igelad,
Tuaregs who today,
in demolition's cycle
and anticyclone of terror,
are burned at Timbuktu
and throughout Aïr, Azawagh,
Ahaggar, Azawad, Ajjer,
to the burst of rockets, flame throwers,
like rats' progeny
of red plague?

Azawad, here's the song
the bitter lament that
the griots of the Sahel and Paris
can't hear,
bitter truth of the conquered!
Yes, between transhumance and combat,
between the Sahara's shores
and the banks of the Niger,
here's the straight naked truth!
We built Timbuktu,
the starting and finishing point,
and we have watched over it since its founding

by the humble servant with her milk gourd and dates
sour as the taste and timber
of our twilight poetry.

Dry eyes, Azawad,
what matters is your vision.
Tell yourself that the tyrants pharaohs emperors
and their heirs will leave one day
and they will soon be pitiless
playthings in the Sahara's whirlwinds.
The sirocco's blast that will scatter them
and their hardware for destruction
like autumn leaves
beyond the wind.
And we will stake our life's visions
upon nothing more than our camel's dung
and the sap of our palm trees.
But, Azawad,
in the fatal and uncertain present,
where the only certainty is
the immeasurable foot of giant chaos
breaking our backs,
departure, it's who we are,
we who depart without hearse or prayer,
we who simply depart
leaving behind us
dust and chicken shit.

March, Azawad,
we're leaving
and one day, the rest will follow us.
But, Azawad,
you and me, we're different

we're already gone,
the nomadic kneecap,
the sons of departure.

Just go, Azawad, don't say farewell to anyone,
for every face you meet
you'll meet again.
Don't take refuge in any face,
yours is ravaged
by rocket's path.

7

Azawad,
the real question isn't
the value of the manuscripts
mosques and saints
that blind the gaze
saddled on Timbuktu's nudity,
nor is it the quota of talons that sting them.
But who sowed fire and bearded wolves
in our goat pens
and then pierced the lamb
with accusing javelin fingers,
metamorphizing
the wandering ewe's son
into wolf sinner?

Azawad, be obstinate.
Hold on,
bite into the fibers of your imagination.
And let go of illusory folklore
of human zoos.
Azawad,
to be defeated is an art
mastered in solitude
in the dark of night.
Defeat is a status apart,
a gaze that ignites thinking,
a vigorous mental faculty
endowed with its own manner of thought

aiming at an ideal with strict demands.
It's an elevated station
situated much higher
than the level of the conquerors.

Azawad,
abandon your worries.
Concern yourself with the immaterial.
Your skeleton is amputated.
Your heart,
they'll make you swallow it.
Your skull is riddled with bullets and worms.
Defend your capital,
the imagination.
Don't ask what's the use
of protecting imaginary goods
since they've turned the brain,
well of reckoning,
into nuclear reactor fuel,
fire burning fires.
In your tongue, Azawad,
the imagination has no measure,
it puts the invisible into view.

Azawad,
the auxiliary forces
of apprentice executioners
who harmoniously tear you apart
with their ogre god
because of your fair complexion
and your eagle nose,
what do they hope to accomplish?
They tear from their shadows

skin and strands of hair
anything reminding them who they were,
self-contempt,
mime chameleons
their pale television reality.
Soon they'll tear their own eyes
from their heads
to screw plastic blue irises
into their empty orbits.

Metropolis, the aunty of Black Africa
has a big job that's far from done.
Sweep the Tuaregs
from every dune and hollow in the Sahara
to populate them with her nephews,
those who can see no further
than their own bellies.

But how long
will it take to refill
the sinkhole abyss
of anomie and domination
that has pierced Africa in the back?
Surely, turning
Tuaregs to cadavers
won't fill the abyss
France dug in Africa's brain.
The Tuareg is skinny
like the grasshopper's paw
and France so greedy that nothing's left
but to furrow ever deeper
into Africa's slit hole.

8

To the south, along your spinal cord,
like the day before yesterday,
the road-roller machines
probe the earth's guts to force its marrow to gush
and to restore the Great War vets,
submachine guns machetes whack-whack
uranium lead enriched armored caskets
for the great destruction
in fire's deluge.

My brother comrade,
companion in agony,
forget about reinforcements
or sales pitches amen salvation!
Beneath the gaping abyss accumulate
silences wails wakes for the dead
screaming writhing
beneath a bed of charring embers
blind machine gun.
Oh arrogant silence,
strangled death rattle, total destruction
stumbling,
shoreless chaos
endless galloping, waste!

Taourirt Amguid Taqourmayes
Ineker Reggan
wonders of progress!

Here's Azawad, stump home of your ruin,
toothless devastation,
desolation of the 1960s,
in the early days
of atomic fire experiments,
jerboas [*gerboises*] nailed to your neck
of real fake stuffed Tuaregs,
wandering scarecrows in the ocean
of radioactive gas radon waves,
errant dead with exiled survivors
on their own occupied land.
Stone Tuareg demon souls,
so long as breath still slouches
and bites the mitered hair
that flees from its own face
in favor of death's?

But as if nothing has happened
outside the body, the breath ventures,
wanders from habit,
sketching a silhouette
that might hover
over its mutilated ghost.
A silhouette for ears alone
or the halo of rising dawn
with stalwart back
under terror's weight.
Terror,
we must defy it!
Terror, Arlit,
lung terror
from French atomic hardware store,
chaos terror
that the artisans and children

mock, hurling
anathemas and obscene gestures
at the reactor's snout,
turd lord of disaster.
And they melt and hammer
the slag and casings
of atomic bombs
for the jewelry and bells
of the betrothed prophetess,
Anzar's betrothed,
lazy rain god
castrated by the burp of an atomic shell
that failed its trial run,
but hit, no doubt,
its true target.

9

Terror disaster!
Azawad,
you're a target.
And behind you,
printed on your back,
it hits me
Tuareg people
with a resisting breath,
reptile insect people
on petrified shell
from radiation
and atomic murders.

Azawad,
you're not only buried alive
your funeral too
is submerged in a flood
of toxic ray chaos waves.

Azawad,
you want to scream,
so howl:
eta emu eja egha alpha.
You, morse code sounds
tingling bacteria amoebas,
brigade of six breaths,
formula for breath's origin,
I hurl you upon echo's flipside,

aghrem alpha egha eja emu eta!
Lend your breath
to mend and strengthen the spine.
Quick, hide eza!
The eza spine is grazed
at the high vertebra,
there at the place we once stood
on the battlefield
where we scorned death,
our fighters hit
to strangle the neck of defeat.

Defeat!
Azawad, don't be afraid
that you'll be forced to spit up your lungs.
It's been a long time, a hundred and nineteen years, Azawad,
since those who destroyed your country
have wanted you dead, unequivocally dead.

But, so far, you're here,
flailing dead,
living dead,
and over there, far away,
you dream that one day
you too will scale the summit,
like our mountain sheep fathers.

But don't imagine you'll find a pothole
underneath the chariot's wheel,
salvation oblivion, where to rest,
innocent prostrate bird
waiting for storm to pass
veering toward distant skies.

No! Azawad.
Chaos is the time
it takes to destroy,
even to destroy the nothingness
that it spawned.
Chaos is the time demanded
by chaos itself.

10

Go, fugitive,
ironic ghost,
burning ghost,
stalk ghost
between fires.
Azawad,
your past silhouette's
blue gray
has vanished in the swell
of hatred and smoke.
Don't moan
nostalgia grief sorrow.
Silence, Azawad!
No one wants to hear you.
Suffocation, asphyxiation,
you're crushed,
dog muzzle in the grave,
trampled strangled.
Azawad,
you must pay
for humanity's cruel appetite,
the price of the rope
placed on your neck.

Pay the price for your Abel eye
in its empty black socket.
Azawad, your garnet gaze
is your twilight,

the only misfortune
that testifies to your solitude
given the defiling of your viscera.
Your land has become your tomb,
your gaze, a trap.
And the immense wealth
in the gut of your land
is your pyre.
So you must
pay the life,
the price for your existence,
sole witness of your death.

Azawad,
your arm isn't long enough,
you have no ammo or voice.
And the big boss knows
only business brutality violence.
Your bent knee and the cost of goods
beneath thunderbolt's ax
won't be enough to save you
at the festival of destruction.
You have no arms or power
to weigh upon the scale of chaos.
And on your face,
the executioner read the lines of defeat,
jagged scars inscribed,
zigzag torch flute
of endurance.
Your name's first grooves
carved between your eyes,
guardians of ruins.

Ceaseless zigzag march,
clandestine march,
resistance's strategy!
Your ancestor's cracked steps
marked you and, before you now,
the path is worn,
straight ahead.

You yourself are the beacon,
lone witness,
mercury's drip,
barbed point
comma thorn
jabbed in
the atom's eye.
You, alone,
in the navel of the volcano,
the end point.
You, Azawad,
you will no longer know
what sleep is.

Go to the innermost part of yourself!
The spark of your self-awareness
doesn't ask for reasons
or how or why
yesterday veils this twilight.
You're surrounded, cornered,
your back is to the squall,
the bullseye
between your brows
is the target,
you alone.

You're alone, Azawad,
without guns or ammo
no allies or comrades in sight.
Your horizon breath
lies between the teeth
of the terror machine,
hash of chewed tendon
for hatred's rumen eaters.

Why, Azawad,
in your mangled locust breast
did you sound the death rattle of your own revolt
on behalf of your own firing squad,
and be called you, too
at the butcher's table?
Is this the lamb's nostalgia for the knife
that itches you?

Don't beg for the very air
you breathe,
shake up your destiny.
Your exterminator
doesn't need your help,
and your soul is already moldy in his teeth.
Hurry up, swarm,
get yourself a corrosive woodworm,
microbe in the ear of your destiny,
subversive bacteria, and plunge headlong
into the ocean of your lonely self.

Azawad,
no ammo,
no speech, they say!
So, turn into varan, your totem

from the Stone Age
who shrunk from giant size
into the exploding coffee grinds of eternity
and shouted to enemy heaven:
"Rock,
under the rock
over the rock!
I am strapped.
Even the wear of time couldn't
unhood me from my newfound shield."

But you, Azawad, you're broken,
you're in the net.
The biscuit,
the only ladle of the ogre,
wrings you in hurricane fire.
And you who suffer,
you've placed your trust in the lord
of your own destruction
rather than the two of us.
You and me, who are equals,
in the face of despair
and self-denial.

Azawad, your ear twitches.
That's because you're still alive.
Every move you make confirms it:
there are no more words,
since bullets ran dry.
But if you say we've spent our words
like bullets
and that anger and despair
now skewer your guts,
then, with stiff joints and spasmic strength,

hold on, hold on tight,
hang on until you can rouse yourself
with the rattle of recognition.
Don't worry,
here's the password
with all the mountain's starch
and resonance.

Temushagha temushagha
temujagha temuzagha
alpha!
Here's the word and the ammo
for hand-to-hand combat.
Your departure's echo, Azawad,
veers toward your motherland ruins.
And so, the burden of resistance
didn't make you swallow your heart
for nothing.
Azawad,
take ant steps
back to yourself, swarm
and pass under nothing's coccyx.

II

The oracles speak to the messengers of the gods.
The messengers of the gods speak
to the era's asses
the age of their ignorance.
And the burnt cricket poets
speak to the burnt illuminated people
their twilight.
Azawad, I tell you this
because they've set you on fire.
You're neither oracle nor messenger,
you're Tuareg poetry,
you wander alone on the open sea,
solitude, resistance.
I too am burnt. I too a firebrand.
Let's cross hell together.

Azawad, I can't save you
from the flaming circle of reprisals.
Poetry isn't a thunderbolt
to fend off atomic strikes.
Azawad, poetry isn't
the shield of an allied brigade
that covers the comrade
helpless cornered demonized people
pursued to fire's ashes,
scape-jackal
target in rifle's scope
for the beaten.

Azawad, poetry can't blunt
the razor-thin rocket
of the remote-controlled guillotine
for those left hanging
on executioner's wall.
No poem will untie
the noose that hangs him to the gallows.
And a poem suspended,
Azawad,
can't turn itself into
a rescue rope
for someone who's been hurled
into the roots of the abyss.
A poem can't
carve a shroud
or build a grave
for an entire nation
impaled on the stake.
Azawad,
poetry has no cash value
to bring capital gains.
Poetry is awkward exhalation
wing, breath,
flashover butterfly
for emotion's epileptic gasps
spanning storms waves flames
chaos anomie devastation.
Butterfly,
Azawad, your gaze must
cut through your tears
ruptures agonies blood and fire
to envision the hazy far shore,
dream, horizon, miraged shore.

Azawad, dissolve the straitjacket,
your self's shape,
in alluring dream gaze
eternal landscape
blue horizon without end
land beyond land
venerated, dream.

Your gaze,
Azawad,
penetrates the kernel of your gaze,
and doesn't look down.
Behind you, boat and moorings
recede to the kingdom of the past,
childhood.

Eza!
Rallying cry
of scapula and shoulders
ripped from thorax.
Crying,
eta eza aa!
Spiraled march
of resistance
where the sky's haunch is carried,
upon the spine,
of endurance
and the earth's pierced basin is hoisted
upon our backs.
It's for you, Azawad, to interrogate
the misery of your self-awareness.
Where do your shackles hurt most,
is it your shoulder blades

or your kidneys?
Azawad,
when restraint's burden
has lanced scab after scab,
from spine to spark seed
your nonnegotiable essence,
it's that the halter ties neck to ankle.

Here, no more antidote
or backward.
Only straight ahead
revolt fury
insurgent roars,
until nerves break free
and your body regains
its subversive rhythm and reversible,
weathervane whirling slingshot head.
Azawad, strike the head
and tyranny's wall
will crumple.

12

Congestion giddiness.
Sated, he seeks a wave trough
to ride ashore, stuffed to the uvula,
the self-cannibalizing hyperogre
belly of the world ship
leans inward.
The turnabout is steep, vertical,
capsizing is eminent!

Azawad,
you, you have no baggage.
Your body is mutilated.
The whole existence of your self
lonely is compressed
in the one bundle
concentrated in your breath
in thread.
Why wait?
Seize hold of your solitary self
panorama on nothingness.

Difficult, Azawad,
the spiraled march!
Pain spasm
spiraled march,
survival cadence Tuareg,
colorless sizzling needle
resonant mosquito sting

that fastens the void's edges
and hitches of distant
and trampled kinsmen,
without dyed drape
of any make or weave.

Azawad, can you hear me
or have you too departed?
If so, why do you let me
call you "Azawad"?
Isn't your name Emazagh,
you, the sunny side of Mauroria Tamazgha,
land of sovereign women mothers?
Go, Emazagh, go now!

The pass at the crossroads is far and steep
for meteorite men and the free winds
of Temuzagha.
Go, Emazagh, go!
I don't advise
you take the vein downstream
for there's no vein left
that hasn't been drained
of blood's deluge.

Upstream, Emazagh,
embrace your pain.
Go on!
You'll reach nerve's source,
row crawl pierce like a gimlet.
Go, Emazagh, it's midnight.
Don't worry who may see you.
There's not a single eye on the horizon.
All is derelict desert plague.

Go on! No one's watching you,
you can leave,
alone.
There's only the void
before you and behind you,
to the right, to the left
up high, down low,
and enemies everywhere.
And you, Emazagh, you are alone.
Loneliness tanned you
with the dregs of the eye
that doesn't see you,
you who are alone.
Go!
The ascent of deserts and mirages
is your heritage, yours alone.

Emazagh,
the goods you've inherited are valuable,
light and easily consumed,
whether you bring them or sell them
except three heavy and difficult treasures
to either squander or preserve:
memory,
self-awareness,
the horizon,
three burdens that are bequeathed to us.

A naked place,
a straight and steep path,
and boundless, infinite, empty horizon.
Naked and radical, this place.
Straight, the trail,
wide and empty, the view

on the horizon of nothingness.
Arid place, bitter trail,
memory of flesh, heritage
of ancestral wakes
of a gaze
grasping its horizon.

The journey is our place, Emazagh,
radical, determined.
We must stay the course
and make ourselves the sons of this place,
as the proverb goes,
until it lies in ruins.

We have a way
and the infinite horizon.
Anyone we meet on the path
can come along, as our comrade
horizon's reaper.
And if he turns out to be our enemy,
we'll put him one day under the horizon.
It's nature, dizziness, truth
of the twilight we must pass through.

Go, Emazagh,
if you're really sure,
you've paid back the credit
that's owed to your self-awareness.
The worst creditor
of them all
is you, yourself.
Go. From the day you were born
domination's saddle has been strapped
upon your back.

Oh mule,
bent under the load
of ancestral pain,
suffocated by the conqueror's vanity.
Go! Set in motion
the spiraled march.
Oh difficult far-off,
high altitude,
capped clavicle horizon
of utopia
set free.

HAWAD, INK 6

The Rinehart Frames
Cheswayo Mphanza
Foreword by Kwame Dawes

Gabriel Okara: Collected Poems
Gabriel Okara
Edited and with an introduction
by Brenda Marie Osbey

Sacrament of Bodies
Romeo Oriogun

The Kitchen-Dweller's Testimony
Ladan Osman
Foreword by Kwame Dawes

Fuchsia
Mahtem Shiferraw

Your Body Is War
Mahtem Shiferraw
Foreword by Kwame Dawes

In a Language That You Know
Len Verwey

Logotherapy
Mukoma Wa Ngugi

When the Wanderers Come Home
Patricia Jabbeh Wesley

*Seven New Generation African
Poets: A Chapbook Box Set*
Edited by Kwame Dawes
and Chris Abani
(Slapering Hol)

*Eight New-Generation African
Poets: A Chapbook Box Set*
Edited by Kwame Dawes
and Chris Abani
(Akashic Books)

*New-Generation African Poets:
A Chapbook Box Set (Tatu)*
Edited by Kwame Dawes
and Chris Abani
(Akashic Books)

*New-Generation African Poets:
A Chapbook Box Set (Nne)*
Edited by Kwame Dawes
and Chris Abani
(Akashic Books)

*New-Generation African Poets:
A Chapbook Box Set (Tano)*
Edited by Kwame Dawes
and Chris Abani
(Akashic Books)

To order or obtain more information on these or other University of
Nebraska Press titles, visit nebraskapress.unl.edu. For more information
about the African Poetry Book Series, visit africanpoetrybf.unl.edu.

OTHER WORKS BY HAWAD

Poetry in French Translation

1985 (1987, 2e édition), *Caravane de la soif*

1987, *Chants de la soif et de l'égarement*

1987 (1989, 2e édition), *Testament nomade*

1989, *L'anneau-sentier*

1991, *Froissevent*

1991, *Yasida*

1992, *La danse funèbre du soleil*

1995, *Sept fièvres et une lune*

1995, *Buveurs de braises*

1998, *Les haleurs d'horizon*

1998, *Le coude grinçant de l'anarchie*

2001, *Notre horizon de gamelles pour une gamelle d'horizons*

2002, *Détournement d'horizon*

Lightning Source UK Ltd.
Milton Keynes UK
UKHW012111040122
396612UK00002B/108